# Umm Barakah

## Stories of the Companions of the Prophet Muhammad for Young Readers

By: Dr. A. Hannibal Hamdallahi, Ph.D

# BLACK HEROES OF ISLAM SERIES

This book is a work of creative storytelling and is intended to educate and inspire young readers about the life of Umm Barakah, one of Prophet Muhammad's closest Companions. It is dedicated to all children who seek courage, faith, and inspiration from the heroes of our past.

First Edition: 2026
Published by Sokoto Publishing
Printed in the United States of America

For information about permissions, special editions, or bulk orders, please contact:
Sokoto Publishing
P.O. Box 280385
Nashville, TN 37228, USA
Email: info@sokotopublishing.com
ISBN: 979-8-9996224-7-1
Text by Dr. A. Hannibal Hamdallahi

Dedication

Since you left, I haven't been the same. May Allah grant you the highest level of Jannah. I look forward to the day I meet God and reunite with you, my dear Brother.

Among the Companions of Prophet Muhammad, there was a beautiful woman named Umm Barakah. Umm Barakah was an African woman from a kingdom called Abyssinia, which is located in present-day Ethiopia. She is special to our Holy Prophet (SAWS) because she served as his governess and guardian when he was very young. Prophet Muhammad described her as his mother after his mother.

Umm Barakah is also special because she was with the Holy Prophet (SAWS) for his entire life. She was there with him when he was first born, and was one of his Companions until he died. Umm Barakah performed the delivery of Prophet Muhammand's birth with his mother Aminah. This makes Umm Barakah the first person in this world to hold the Prophet in her beautiful, warm, and nurturing Black arms. Umm Barakah was given the special honor of being the first person in the world to physically touch the Messenger of Allah (SAWS). This is an honor that Black woman all over the world should cherish.

The first person to smile at Rasool Allah (SAWS), and to embrace the beauty and adorableness of Rasool Allah (SAWS), was a Black woman.

Umm Barakah also had the special responsibility to contribute to Prophet Muhammad's (SAWS) social and moral upbringing. She played a large role in the development of Prophet Muhammad's (SAWS) character and conduct. She made sure that he ate his vegetables and fruit, she ensured he received enough sleep at night, and that he developed healthy habits of hygiene and cleanliness.

وَإِنَّكَ لَعَلَىٰ خُلُقٍ عَظِيمٍ

## "And you are truly a man of outstanding character."
### - Qu'ran 68:4

Umm Barakah was present at every single battle fought by the Holy Prophet (SAWS), including the important battle of Uhud. During this battle, things got a bit challenging for the Muslim army. Many of them began to flee, and left Prophet Muhammad (SAWS) vulnerable to the enemy. At this important moment, Umm Barakah was one of the women who picked up a sword and came to the Prophet's (SAWS) aide. She helped to surround the Prophet (SAWS) while wielding her sword and defended the Holy Prophet (SAWS) with her own life.

Umm Barakah also migrated from Mecca to Medinah with Prophet Muhammad (SAWS). It's narrated that at one of the rest stops during this long journey, she was extremely thirsty and fatigued in the hot desert. Because she was fasting, her physical strength was even further weakened. As she was losing energy and strength due to extreme thirst, a container of water with a white rope was sent down to her from the sky. Umm Baraka said that, "I took it and drank it until I was satisfied. I never felt any thirst after that. I had exposed myself to thirst through fasting in hot days but I did not feel thirsty." This miracle shows the love that Allah demonstrated towards Umm Barakah and His mercy for those who follow the Holy Prophet (SAWS).

Umm Barakah was also the mother of Usama ibn Zayd – another important African companion of Prophet Muhammad (SAWS). When Usama ibn Zayd was only 18 years, Prophet Muhammad (SAWS) gave him full and complete control of a force sent to attack the Byzantine Empire. Some of the older men and veterans of previous wars balked at Usama ibn Zayd's new position. They believed him to be too young to have command over them. In response to this, it's narrated that Prophet Muhammad (SAWS) said, "I have been informed that you spoke about Usama. (Let it be known that) he is the most beloved of all people to me." Thus, even the son of Umm Barakah was among the most beloved people to Rasool Allah (SAWS). This shows that Umm Barakah was very careful with the way she raised people in her care.

Prophet Muhammad (SAWS) showed great respect and admiration for Umm Barakah. He would often pay social visits to her house and enjoy the company of her entire family. Prophet Muhammad (SAWS) loved Umm Barakah and so did his Companions. In fact, when the Prophet (SAWS) passed away, Abu Bakr and Umar (May Allah be pleased with them both) would still go and visit her because they loved her, and they knew the Prophet (SAWS) loved her dearly as well.

When Prophet Muhammad (SAWS) died, they found her crying. They asked, why are you crying? The Prophet is now with Allah, and that's a beautiful thing. She told them, "That's not why I'm crying...I'm crying because the revelations from the heavens have stopped." This statement encapsulates her life in a nutshell. She was a true believer in Allah and in His Holy Messenger (SAWS). Her faith in Allah did not falter with the passing of the Holy Prophet (SAWS), rather, it only increased and became more determined.

May Allah bless Umm Barakah, and may we all continue to learn great lessons from the remarkable life she led in the cause of Allah.